The Measurement of Property, Plant, and Equipment in Financial Statements

PARTICIPANTS

ANDREW BARR, Chief Accountant
Securities and Exchange Commission

ALBERT Y. BINGHAM, Financial Vice President
Chicago Title and Trust Company

GEORGE T. CONKLIN, JR., Vice President
Guardian Life Insurance Company of America

SIDNEY DAVIDSON, Professor
The University of Chicago

THOMAS D. FLYNN, Partner
Arthur Young & Company

PAUL GRADY, Partner
Price Waterhouse & Co.

LAWRENCE C. HORNOR, Controller
Nashua Corporation

ERIC L. KOHLER, Chicago

DONALD F. MACEACHERN, Chief Accountant
American Telephone and Telegraph Company

CARL L. NELSON, Professor
Columbia University

JOHN W. QUEENAN, Partner
Haskins & Sells

PHILLIP L. WEST, Vice President
New York Stock Exchange

MODERATOR

ROBERT N. ANTHONY, Professor
Harvard Graduate School of Business Administration

CONSULTANTS

IRMA ADELMAN, Associate Professor of Political Economy
The Johns Hopkins University

ETTORE BARBATELLI
American Appraisal Company

Foreword

Among the basic functions of a university are the dissemination of knowledge and the addition to knowledge. The Accounting Round Table, reported in this book, does not fit neatly into either category. Its purpose was not to teach students; indeed, no students were permitted at any of the discussions. Neither did it have a research purpose, in the usual meaning of the word research. A voluminous literature already exists on the topic discussed, and those who instigated the Round Table did not believe that additional research — either of the fact-finding, or the experimental, or the model building, or the analytical types — would provide fruitful additions to this store of knowledge.

The original proposal for the round table put it this way:

> There are a number of important unresolved questions in accounting, but they are not problems for which the best solutions can be arrived at by research. Arguments about these issues are aired in numerous books and articles and at numerous meetings. No issues are resolved by written arguments even when accompanied by written rejoinders. Meetings, even with discussion, do not provide an effective way of coming to grips with an issue, partly because they do not allow enough time for a really thorough discussion and partly because the participants are not chosen in such a way that the best thinking available is focused on the problem. The usual "panel discussion," for example, may

bring together two or three good people, but their formal remarks are usually brief and often not quite on the same point, the ensuing discussion is impeded by irrelevancies thrown in from the audience, and the whole thing is over in two or three hours at most.

The proposal was, therefore, that we invite a small group whose members represented a variety of points of view on a significant accounting problem, and that this group would discuss the problem in some depth. The topic of the measurement of property, plant, and equipment was selected for the first such discussion.

You will note that the list of participants includes men who are responsible for the preparation of financial statements; men from insurance companies and banks who use the information contained in these statements; men from the public accounting profession; men associated with regulatory agencies; and men from the academic community. We believe that in a discussion of this kind it is wise to have the viewpoints of all these segments of society. I should point out that, after discussion with the American Institute of Certified Public Accountants, it was decided that it would be best not to invite men who were currently members of the Accounting Principles Board.

We are grateful for the support that the Round Table idea has received. In particular, we are grateful to the participants. They are busy men, and they understood that participation involved not only two full days of discussion at the Round Table meeting, but also many hours of preparatory reading and many hours of reading and commenting on drafts of this report.

Funds for this project were furnished by the Arthur Young Foundation. We appreciate not only the money but also the spirit in which it was given. The donors agreed that we should make the decisions on the selection of participants, the conduct of the Round Table, and the publication of its results. At no point did they indicate any desire to stray from this agreement.

From the Business School staff, Professor Robert N. Anthony originated the idea and served as moderator, and Dr. Robert T. Sprouse performed the extremely intricate job of selecting, condensing, arranging, and reporting the key points that emerged from the discussion. Assistant Professor David F. Hawkins was in charge of arrangements.

Members of the Round Table have read and commented on drafts of this summary report. However, any group will quite naturally differ among themselves as to the best choice of language or emphasis in a summary report of this kind. We emphasize, therefore, that the responsibility for the report itself rests on Dr. Sprouse, the reporter, not on individual participants in the Round Table.

George P. Baker
DEAN

Table of Contents

I | Introduction

In April 1963 a group of distinguished accounting practitioners, scholars, users and providers of accounting information, and public officials met in Dedham, Massachusetts, to discuss the significant issues involved in the measurement of property, plant, and equipment in financial statements. This is a report of that meeting.

OBJECTIVES AND COMPOSITION

A great deal of attention has been focused on the measurement of property, plant, and equipment during the last fifteen years. Such measurement has a direct and significant effect on the determination of income as well as on the determination of financial position. In addition, the subject is important because it continues to be one of the most controversial areas encountered in the preparation and interpretation of financial statements. Historical acquisition costs remain virtually the only valuation basis used, but a variety of proposals for change have appeared in the literature, and in rare cases departures from historical cost — either appraisal values or replacement costs — have been adopted for reporting purposes with the approval of the auditors.[1] In some cases in which provisions for "price-level depreciation" or other price level adjustments have been reported, the

---

[1] For example, Creole Petroleum Corporation, which is incorporated in Delaware but operates in Venezuela, and Imperial Tobacco Company of Canada, Ltd. Both companies are listed on the American Stock Exchange.

auditors have been careful to point out that such provisions were *not* within the scope of generally accepted accounting principles, but at the same time they have asserted that the results were "more fairly presented" after such adjustments had been made.[2]

There also is other evidence of concern with the problem. Some businessmen have asserted that the measurement of depreciation on the basis of historical cost tends to overstate income — that a tax on such income is in part a tax on capital and that dividends based on such income could be distributions of capital.

The primary objective of the Round Table was to discuss the significant issues surrounding various methods of accounting for property, plant, and equipment and the relevant arguments regarding each. From the outset, it was agreed that members of the Round Table would not attempt to resolve these issues or issue a recommendation. It also was agreed that anything that was said in the course of the discussions would be neither identified with the individual who said it nor weighted by the number who agreed or disagreed. Accordingly, no votes were taken. Similarly, in this summary of the discussion no attempt is made to identify who or how many among the members of the Round Table supported the various alternatives or supported the individual arguments that were presented, pro and con, in the course of the discussion.

It was hoped that this freedom from any need to make a group recommendation would permit the Round Table to make a special contribution to the problem area. All too often group recommendations are the product of compromises. And compromises are likely to obscure the most crucial issues, rather than to isolate and emphasize them.

---

[2] For example, Ayrshire Collieries Corporation, listed on the American Stock Exchange, and Iowa-Illinois Gas and Electric Company, listed on the New York Stock Exchange.

The Round Table membership was selected to include a variety of points of view. The resolution of the problems of financial reporting is not the exclusive domain of the public accounting profession. Indeed, proposed solutions can be effectively implemented only with the support of the three major groups concerned — *managements,* who have the primary responsibility for financial reports; *investors and other users,* whose information needs are the very reason for issuing financial reports; and *certified public accountants,* whose unqualified opinions about financial statements are accepted as assurance that the financial statements fairly present financial positions and results of operations in accordance with generally accepted accounting principles. The diversity of background and viewpoint represented in the Round Table's membership is much greater than that in any single professional organization. The individual members were selected as individuals, not as representatives of their employers or of any organizations.

PROCEDURE

In order to facilitate the Round Table discussions, an Advance Document (see Appendix B) was prepared and distributed to participants before the Dedham meeting. This document contained (1) a suggested definition of the problem, (2) suggested criteria for judging alternative proposals, and (3) summaries of various proposals for fixed asset accounting that have been made from time to time.

The Round Table devoted the first morning to a careful delineation of the question on which the discussion would focus and to establishment of appropriate criteria for evaluating proposals. These discussions are summarized in Chapter II, Statement of the Problem, and Chapter III, Criteria. The suggestions contained in the advance document served as a point of departure for these discussions; the discussion summaries in Chapters

II and III reflect the Round Table's amendments, deletions, and additions to those suggestions.

Two technical experts were invited to meet with the Round Table during the first afternoon. Professor Irma Adelman, Associate Professor of Political Economy at The Johns Hopkins University, discussed the construction, use, and interpretation of price indexes. Mr. Ettore Barbatelli, American Appraisal Company, New York, discussed the conduct, meaning, and feasibility of valuation of property, plant, and equipment by appraisal. In keeping with the spirit of the Round Table, the two experts expressed their personal views and responded to questions and views of members of the Round Table. The consultations with Professor Adelman and Mr. Barbatelli are not reported separately. However, to the extent that the subsequent discussions were influenced by their testimony, the summaries of the Round Table discussions reflect the results of those consultations.

During the entire second day the Round Table focused its attention directly on answers to the central question: At what amount should property, plant, and equipment be shown on published balanced sheets? These discussions were dominated by the consideration of the prevailing practice of accounting for historical acquisition costs and three proposed alternatives — adjustments for general price-level changes, market value, and replacement cost.

Chapters IV through VII provide a brief sketch of each concept considered and also summarize the crucial considerations — favorable and unfavorable to each — as they emerged in the course of the discussions. In addition, statements of the same or related proposals as they appeared in the advance document are included in Appendix B.

It is noteworthy, perhaps, that discussions of at least two other bases for the valuation of property, plant, and equipment were specifically rejected by the Round Table

ROBERT N. ANTHONY, Moderator

ROBERT T. SPROUSE, Reporter, and
DAVID F. HAWKINS, in Charge of Arrangements

ROBERT N. ANTHONY with ETTORE BARBATELLI and IRMA ADELMAN, Consultants

because their inherent deficiencies in terms of both feasibility and objectivity were such that thorough consideration was deemed unwarranted. The rejected concepts were the determination of economic value and reliance upon appraisals as a general approach to either market value or replacement cost. The advance statement of each of these proposals is reproduced in Appendix B.

NATURE OF THIS SUMMARY

As already stated, the purpose of the Round Table was to illuminate issues, not to resolve them. This summary is written in the same spirit. It is not a "transcript," or "proceedings," or a "sense of the meeting," much less a recommendation for action. It attempts to set forth all the points of view that emerged in the discussion, without indicating who or how many supported each. Thus, the reader can be assured that at least one person supported each point described herein, but he should attempt no inference as to how widespread the support was.

In order to give the flavor of the discussion, we have used a number of quotations from the transcript of the Round Table, but these are not identified with the people making them.

II | Statement of the Problem

The central issue on which the Round Table focused its attention was this: *At what amount should property, plant, and equipment be shown on published balance sheets?* In order to insure that this central question would be faced squarely and thoroughly in the limited though substantial period of time available, it was necessary that it be clearly circumscribed. Accordingly, certain suggestions for delineating the question were set forth in the advance document. These were considered by the Round Table and the following clarifications and limitations on the discussion emerged:

First, the phrase "property, plant, and equipment" was limited to those *tangible assets held by a business enterprise for the purpose of producing and distributing goods and services.* Accordingly, it embraced land, buildings, machinery, and items of equipment, including fixtures, delivery vehicles, tools, dies and patterns, etc. Intangible assets were specifically excluded, as were tangible assets that were held primarily for sale or investment.

With the exception of land, the tangible assets with which the Round Table was concerned are those with a limited useful life. Their life is limited by their capability of rendering useful economic services although their physical substance may be virtually unchanged. They do not become physically embodied in the products they help to create. This latter characteristic dif- ferentiates property, plant, and equipment from inventories and wasting assets that become exhausted as they are physically incorporated into a product.

Second, attention was concentrated on the measurement of assets in those *financial statements with respect to which certified public accountants render their opinions* concerning fair presentation "in conformity with generally accepted accounting principles." It was assumed that bases and procedures used by individual companies for internal reporting and decision-making purposes need not be restricted by what is considered to be proper accounting in financial reports to outsiders. Similarly, it was assumed that conclusions with respect to general purpose financial reports to outsiders need not affect those financial reports that are designed to meet the special and perhaps unique needs of specific external recipients, e.g., to conform with explicit regulatory or contractual requirements.

The questions of whether certain information contained in internal reports would be useful to outsiders or whether financial reports submitted to regulatory agencies should be the same as financial statements provided to investors and other interested segments of the general public were expressly excluded from the discussions. It was recognized that internal financial reports and special purpose financial reports need not necessarily be restricted by conformity to generally accepted accounting principles, whereas it is crucial that financial reports intended for investors or the general public be standardized to the extent that they do conform to generally accepted accounting principles.

Third, the discussion was limited to the data in those *financial statements (including footnotes) embraced by the certified public accountant's opinion.* Accordingly, the desirability of additional information that might be supplied voluntarily — either in "presidents' letters" or in the form of supplementary schedules or statements — was not considered.

solution to the broader one. To use the alternative approach would require the group to consider such diverse topics as inventories, intercorporate investments, and intangible assets, as well as property, plant, and equipment. Such consideration would have been likely to result in a diffusion of efforts.

Eighth and finally, it was assumed that, for the purpose of this discussion, *there should be only one basic principle for the measurement of property, plant, and equipment that would apply to all but specified exceptional situations.* The purpose of this assumption was to sharpen the focus of the discussion. To admit the possibility of equally acceptable alternatives would tend to gloss over differences of opinion as to which alternative actually is preferred.

Focusing on a single, basic principle does not rule out the reporting of dual information — say, *both* historical acquisition cost *and* a determinable current value, or *both* unadjusted historical acquisition cost *and* historical acquisition cost adjusted for general price level changes — particularly during a period of transition. The single, basic principle assumption means only that a free choice of one of two or more significantly different alternative accounting principles was not acceptable for purposes of the Round Table discussion. Of course, recognition of a single, basic principle with respect to the financial statements in no way restricts the voluntary presentation of interpretive supplementary material.

Neither does the single, basic principle assumption mean that, regardless of differences in situations and availability of facts, there should be a single method or procedure for implementing that principle. For example, if the basic principle for estimating depreciation were to be related to the expiration of economic benefits or service potential, this principle might properly be implemented by the straight-line method in some situations and by an accelerated method in other situations.

Much professional judgment always will be involved in the application of basic principles. The precise circumstances under which transactions occur are seldom if ever alike. The assumption of a single, basic principle means that when situations are alike — when the facts are similar and known — application of the single principle tends toward a single solution. However, it is recognized that situations are seldom exactly alike; so in practice this must be regarded as a tendency only.

III | Criteria

In an attempt to identify the significant issues involved in the measurement of property, plant, and equipment for financial statement purposes, it seemed desirable that each proposal under serious consideration be evaluated on the basis of a set of fundamental criteria. To arrive at a conclusion it might be necessary to attach more importance to certain criteria than to others, but presumably any proposal that failed completely to satisfy any one of the criteria would be unacceptable. The following criteria were proposed in the advance document and are presented here as modified to reflect the Round Table's comments:

(1) *Objectivity.*[3] The importance of objectivity in financial accounting is widely acknowledged. Indeed, the assertion of objectivity has always had an overwhelming influence on financial theory and practice, and rightly so. Although this criterion and the underlying reasons for it often are not explicitly set forth, the crux of objectivity is identified with two related requirements: (a) financial accounting information should be presented according to certain standards and (b) verification of

---

[3] In Eric L. Kohler's *A Dictionary for Accountants* (Englewood Cliffs, N.J., Prentice Hall, Inc., 1963, 3rd edition), page 340, the term "objective" is defined as "having a meaning or application apart from the investigator, the peculiarities of his experience, or of the environment, and substantiated or capable of being substantiated by the findings of independent investigators."

financial accounting information should be feasible.

It is generally recognized that financial statements are the representations of management. The independent auditor's responsibility is confined to the expression of a professional opinion on the financial statements he has examined. In an important sense, however, published financial statements are reports *on* management; such reports can be meaningful only if there are objective methods of verifying their contents.

Within the confines of generally accepted accounting principles, managerial judgments may enter the accounting process directly. For example, in the case of depreciable assets, management's responsibility is to estimate the useful lives of assets and adopt rational and consistent methods of amortization during those lives. Both of these actions involve judgments. At the very least, however, such judgments are subject to the test of reasonableness. If management were permitted complete latitude within the extremes of writing off a long but limited-lived asset at the time of acquisition or refraining from amortizing it at all, the usefulness of financial statements would be effectively nullified. Accordingly, when the independent auditor renders an unqualified opinion about financial statements, the user should be entitled to assume with confidence (a) that such information fairly reflects management's business decisions and methods of accounting, not whatever management chooses to report about the results following from those decisions, and (b) that the independent auditor has sufficiently satisfied himself as to the existence of the business transactions reflected in the financial statements and has considered the reasonableness of reporting their effects.

The criterion of objectivity is relative rather than absolute. Clearly we are willing to give up some degree of objectivity in exchange for an increase in usefulness. Take land as an example. Probably the most objective information about a piece of land is its physical size. To report "100 acres" of land is more objective than to report land "(at cost) $100,000," because the latter figure involves some judgment as to which outlays were properly included in the cost. The phrase "100 acres" of land is not so useful as a description, however; the land in question may be under water, arid, mountainous, or in the center of a thriving city.

It is even more obvious that to report "one building" and "one acre of land" is more objective than to allocate the single purchase price for land and the building on it between land and building, and subsequently to refer to those allocations as "the cost" of land and "the cost" of the building. But there are many situations in which it is necessary, in the interest of usefulness, to make such allocations of the cost of a "basket purchase" to the various elements acquired.

No one seriously questions the practice of recording depreciation during the useful life of depreciable assets, although a subjective judgment of that useful life is required. It is a judgment that cannot be fully verified because the useful life is dependent upon the future and the future is uncertain. It is futile, therefore, to insist upon *absolute* objectivity. On the other hand, *some degree* of objectivity is essential and it is reasonable to demand that any relaxation in objectivity be offset by an increase in usefulness.

(2) *Usefulness.* Audited financial statements are intended to provide reliable information to appropriately interested parties. With the separation of management and ownership, management's responsibility for satisfying the informational requirements of outsiders has been accentuated.

Usefulness, however, is an abstract concept and can be applied meaningfully as a criterion only when responsive to such questions as "useful to whom?" and "useful for what purpose?" Information that is useful to management in making its decisions is not necessarily useful to stockholders in arriving at their investment decisions.

As indicated earlier, information that may be useful to the Internal Revenue Service in the administration of federal taxes may be of little use to other parties.

There is considerable precedent for identifying the primary users of published financial statements as the investor group.[4] This is a natural and logical outgrowth of the securities legislation that has been so effective in stimulating increased availability and improved quality of financial information.

For the purposes of the Round Table discussion, the criterion of usefulness was applied in the sense of *usefulness to investors who are willing and competent to read financial statements carefully and with discrimination for the purposes of assistance in arriving at rational investment decisions.* Even if a broader point of view were favored — if usefulness were to be assessed in terms of the interest of the general public — it seems unlikely that the interests of investors and of the public would conflict.

---

[4] The introduction to "Accounting Research Bulletin No. 43" explicitly recognizes that:

". . . The problems in the field of accounting have increasingly come to be considered from the standpoint of the buyer or seller of an interest in an enterprise, with consequent increased recognition of the significance of the income statement and a tendency to restrict narrowly charges and credits to surplus. The fairest possible presentation of periodic net income, with neither material overstatement nor understatement, is important, since the results of operations are significant not only to prospective buyers of an interest in the enterprise but also to prospective sellers. With the increasing importance of the income statement there has been a tendency to regard the balance sheet as the connecting link between successive income statements; however, this concept should not obscure the fact that the balance sheet has significant uses of its own." American Institute of Certified Public Accountants (AICPA), Committee on Accounting Procedure, *Restatement and Revision of Accounting Research Bulletins.* Accounting Research Bulletin No. 43 (New York, AICPA, 1953), p. 7.

The American Accounting Association's Committee on Concepts and Standards agrees:

(3) *Feasibility.* In order to merit serious consideration, valuation bases must be capable of practicable and economic implementation. Proposals that, although theoretically sound and desirable, are nevertheless obviously impossible to attain under ordinary conditions, may be rejected summarily. On the other hand, one must not conclude that comparisons of feasible proposals with some theoretical ideal are sterile. Such comparisons frequently may be useful as a means of analysis and evaluation. The sacrifice involved in accepting something less than an ideal also may be relevant.

Similarly, proposals are unacceptable that are possible of attainment but only at a cost that is clearly disproportionate to any additional benefits relative to less costly alternatives. This is a fundamental economic principle that hardly needs elaboration.

It was assumed by the Round Table that if any change from current practice were proposed, its adoption would not be unduly precipitate. However, the Round Table was not concerned with appropriate transitional procedures; a period of systematic transition, if any, was taken for granted.

The standard form of auditor's opinion uses the phrase

"The potential users of corporate reports include governmental agencies, short- and long-term creditors, labor organizations, stockholders, and potential investors. Since in all likelihood the needs of these groups cannot be served equally well by a single set of statements, the interest of some one audience should be identified as primary. Traditionally, this has been the stockholder group.

"In view of the facts that short-term creditors and governmental administrative agencies will typically have the power to require information specific to their purposes and that no important differences in the basic informational requirements of the other interests cited seem to exist, the traditional emphasis on the requirements of the stockholder group appears to be sound...." American Accounting Association, Committee on Concepts and Standards Underlying Corporate Financial Statements, "Standards of Disclosure for Published Financial Reports," Supplementary State-

"fairly presents . . . in conformity with generally accepted accounting principles." "Fairness" has been suggested as *the* basic postulate of accounting. The concept of fairness as used in the auditor's opinion, however, is related to a particular standard applied to the facts presented — namely, adequate disclosure and conformity with generally accepted principles of accounting applied on a consistent basis — and not to variable philosophies of individuals. Any broader concept of fairness raises many of the same questions that were raised above in reference to usefulness, that is, "fair to whom?" and "fair for what purpose?" Although the terminology chosen is different, it is assumed that the broad concept of fairness is encompassed by the criterion of usefulness, or, if not separately, by the combination of the objectivity and usefulness criteria.

---

ment No. 8, *The Accounting Review,* Vol. XXX (July 1955), p. 401.

The Committee on Concepts and Standards stressed another point that was pertinent to the Round Table's endeavor:

"The conclusion that financial statements should provide data necessary for sound investor decisions does not imply that every investor or potential investor will be able to make full use of this information without technical assistance. A business firm of even moderate size is a complex mechanism the activities of which are not susceptible to simple explanation. . . .

"No implication is here intended that published reports should be geared to the specifications of the expert analyst. On the contrary, we hold . . . that it should 'be possible for a person moderately experienced in business and finance to obtain from such statements basic information on which he may rely with confidence.'" (*Ibid.,* pp. 401-402.)

JOHN W. QUEENAN,
Partner
Haskins & Sells

DONALD F. MACEACHERN,
Chief Accountant
*American Telephone and
Telegraph Company*

GEORGE T. CONKLIN, JR
Vice President
*Guardian Life
Insurance Company of Am*

ALBERT Y. BINGHAM,
Financial Vice President
*Chicago Title and Trust
Company*

CARL L. NELSON, Professor
Columbia University

PAUL GRADY, Partner
Price Waterhouse & Co

PHILIP L. WEST,
Vice President
w York Stock Exchange

LAWRENCE C. HORNOR,
Controller
Nashua Corporation

ANDREW BARR,
Chief Accountant
*Securities and
Exchange Commission*

NEY DAVIDSON, Professor
he *University of Chicago*

ERIC L. KOHLER, Chicago

THOMAS D. FLYNN,
Partner
*Arthur Young &
Company*

IV | Historical Acquisition Cost

The nature of historical acquisition cost and its peculiar attributes are well known. Generally, the historical acquisition cost of an item of property, plant, and equipment is the sum of all costs incurred in getting the item in condition and location ready for use. Because such costs tend to be the result of bargained exchanges, historical acquisition costs may be viewed as significant because they represent *prima facie* evidence of economic value at time of acquisition. They may also be viewed as significant as measures of amounts committed by management to specific purposes or resources. Historical acquisition costs are measured in terms of dollars at the date of acquisition; subsequent changes in the general purchasing power of dollars and changes in the prices of specific assets are ignored.

SUMMARY OF ROUND TABLE DISCUSSION

(1) *Is accounting for historical acquisition costs objective and feasible?*

Currently the prevailing basis for accounting for items of property, plant, and equipment is their historical acquisition cost. The fact that financial statements have usually been prepared on this basis is incontrovertible evidence of *feasibility*, and one of the major strengths attributed to the use of historical acquisition costs is the *objectivity* with which they may be determined.

"I have a very strong disposition to look with favor on historical cost because of the objectivity factor. Using that as a yardstick, I don't like to give that up unless there is a definite benefit which can be clearly gained from using some alternative method."

"As an advantage of historical cost, availability of data without additional cost may be added to objectivity."

"It might be pointed out that historical acquisition costs are not as subject to manipulation as some other valuations would likely be."

(2) *Is accounting for historical acquisition costs useful?*

Proposals for conversion to some other basis are inevitably asserted as a means whereby the usefulness of accounting information would be improved or augmented; the advocates of such proposals therefore challenge the *usefulness* of historical cost information.

"I am inclined to think that neither the balance sheet nor the income statement prepared on the basis of historical costs gives a figure that is of any significance."

Nevertheless, some uses of historical cost information were advanced.

"Financial statements based on historical costs are part of the discipline of management. . . . It is part of their responsibility to the public to show what has been invested in the business and where that investment has gone, regardless of the fact that price levels may have changed radically over the period of time that this capital has been invested."

"Everyone who is opposed to historical cost valuation of assets has opposed it primarily because it gives us improper depreciation figures."

"Cost represents that portion of the investment that has been expended on fixed assets, whereas the depreciation expense on the same basis appearing in the income statement represents that portion of those expenditures that has been amortized. I don't think there is any other main significance to the figures than that — but that is extremely significant — a first hand value to investors as well as others."

"To measure expenses in terms of dollars is to measure income in terms of dollars. Many companies have obligations payable in dollars. Payment of these obligations requires dollars. If a firm has sufficient income (in dollars), it can pay these debts regardless of price movements. If we measure income in some other way and prices fall, a firm could operate with a large income and yet become insolvent."

". . . if you take any schedule of historical information, it is subject to a very great deal of analysis and out of this you can conclude quite definitely whether an enterprise is managed well or poorly."

"It is valuable as a history of what has happened in the company and therefore can be used as an analytical tool. However, it does seem to me to have very limited usefulness and therefore it would be desirable for the accounting profession to provide additional information of some nature which would particularly improve current comparability among companies."

Even if it is felt that there are significant limitations in the usefulness of historical cost, the greater usefulness attributed by advocates of alternative bases of measurement may be unconvincing, particularly when weighed against the degree of objectivity that might be sacrificed. Indeed, for some, the continued primary use of historical acquisition costs may be supported not so much out of the conviction that the resultant information fulfills the needs of users as out of a conviction that alternatives tend to be even less desirable.

"This isn't very good, but we haven't got anything better."

"It is the most objective thing we have."

"It is a good starting point for many types of analysis. It is the one anchor that you have that is helpful."

It is generally acknowledged that the use of historical acquisition costs for property, plant, and equipment has convention and experience in its favor. Clearly, therefore, if a different basis is to be adopted, its advantages must be effectively demonstrated. The burden of persuasion rests with those who advocate changes.

"The fact that contracts are made for the payment of dollars — and long term contracts at that — indicates that businessmen think that dollars are significant. Accounting reports are made to the business community (which includes investors) and such reports should be in terms that are important to this group."

"The reason that I feel so strongly about continuing historical cost is that I see no reason whatever for making a change. Why should we make a change?"

Perhaps one of the factors most favorable to the continued use of historical acquisition cost is the widespread recognition that the reported amounts do *not* represent value — that they merely reflect unexpired cost. Representations that amounts in financial statements represent value may be grossly misleading. Values change from day to day, and the erroneous assumption might arise that the balance sheet represents the amount that could be obtained upon liquidation.

> "One of the real factors in favor of the historical cost is that it has been generally accepted to be *not* a value figure — merely an accounting figure. That has great importance with respect to what people expect to get out of financial statements."

(3) *Should historical cost information be eliminated entirely if other methods of valuation are adopted?*

Many who favor disclosure of the effects of changes in the general price level would not wish to eliminate the reporting of data based on historical acquisition costs. Even if price level information were to be required, perhaps it could be provided effectively in adjunct accounts or in supplementary and coordinate statements.

> "I think it would be a mistake to do away with the historical financial statements, but coordinate statements adjusted for price-level changes would be tremendously helpful."

> ". . . the books certainly should be stated in historical cost and historical cost should be displayed in the financial statements. But it should be compulsory to also show general price-level adjustments in published financial statements."

On the other hand, those who favor some form of current value (e.g., market value or replacement cost) tend to be less impressed with the relevance of simultaneous reporting of historical acquisition costs.

"I am not sure what we mean when we say that we wish to keep historical cost. When we can get the figure we really want to show, I would not attach any special significance to historical cost — at least not after we have completed the transitional period."

(4) *Does accounting for historical cost fulfill the objectives of financial accounting?*

Some view accounting primarily as the recording and reporting of transactions that have actually been experienced by a business firm.

"Accounting is no more than the recording and reporting of transactions. . . . This conference hasn't convinced me in the slightest that accounting is anything more than that. In fact, it confirms that notion. Transactions are what we are reporting on — past experience, past events that have actually taken place, conditions that have arisen in the past."

As such, it is argued that there is no inconsistency in having a machinery account, for example, summarizing a hundred items, each item representing the same type of machine, but purchased at different times at different prices. Once incurred, historical costs do not change. Valuations other than historical cost, however, are evanescent — they change from year to year and with various points of view.

"Sometimes you find as many points of view about what values should be as there are persons."

It may be suggested that, if it is believed that reported earnings include an erosion of capital, then the retained earnings account should be allowed to accumulate and surplus reserves be created.

"If it means that surplus reserves and accumulation of earned surplus solve the problems created by inflation, I disagree."

It is argued that if there is reason to believe that different methods of valuation may provide useful information, such information may be disclosed in footnotes attached to the statements that are prepared on the basis of historical cost.

V | Historical Acquisition Cost Adjusted for General Price-Level Changes

SUMMARY OF ROUND TABLE DISCUSSION

Adjustments to historical acquisition costs to reflect changes in the general price level are advocated as a method of providing a measurement of investments in assets and their expiration in terms of the amount of general purchasing power invested and expiring. It is readily acknowledged that unadjusted dollars represent varying amounts of purchasing power at various times. This being the case, the practice in financial statements of adding, subtracting, and comparing the dollars of different years has been questioned by some. Price level adjustments convert dollars of different years and different purchasing power to a measuring unit of the same general purchasing power; accounts are restated in terms of current dollars having the same purchasing power.

> "The reason why I am interested in using the general price-level index is to develop a stable measuring unit. If deflation takes place — fine — let's apply the same principle to record the effects of deflation as well as inflation — or the effects of a continuing stable price level with respect to the changes that took place in the past and are still being reflected in the current statements."

The monetary unit of the country in which business is

conducted has generally served as the common denominator in the field of accounting. In the United States, of course, this has been the dollar. Those in favor of general price level adjustments consider this practice satisfactory only while there are no major changes in the purchasing power of the monetary unit. They suggest that continued use of unadjusted dollars in the face of price level changes is analogous to the use of a yardstick that varies in length from year to year. Adjustments that reflect change in the purchasing power of the dollar are therefore advocated as a means by which the length of the yardstick can be standardized.

Adjustments for general price-level changes are not advocated as a method of determining the value of an asset or the replacement cost of an asset. They are intended only to state the historical acquisition costs of assets in terms of a current and common monetary unit. Typically, in estimating depreciation, the accountant attempts to spread the cost of an asset over its useful life; he deals neither with value nor with replacement cost, but rather with the dollars actually invested in the asset. General price-level adjustments are intended to provide an expression of that cost in the same dollars as those in which sales, wages, and most expense items are expressed.

> "I shudder at trying to set up value on a balance sheet. What I am talking about is original cost or historical cost adjusted for changes in the size of the dollar. This has nothing to do with value. There is no question of trying to find an index that will represent the change in the replacement cost of something."

(1) *Can adjustments for changes in the general price level be feasible and objective?*

Those favoring price level adjustments have little doubt that it is feasible to adjust financial statements for changes in the general price level with the same degree of objectivity that now exists with respect to conventional statements. They also recognize that the effects of price level changes are not confined to property, plant, and equipment. It is argued by some that if price level adjustments are to be made, they should be made comprehensively, measuring the impact on each account affected. But, although the specific problem before the Round Table was restricted to accounting for property, plant, and equipment, consideration of price level adjustments was appropriate, inasmuch as the alleged inadequacies of financial statements based on unadjusted historical acquisition costs are often most significant in the case of long-lived assets and their amortization.

"We can get a statement on a general price level basis by adjusting all items by the GNP Implicit Price Deflator that is just as objective — just as reliable — as our historical cost statements."

"For whatever use the historic cost is, the general price-level adjusted cost is better in that it brings us that much closer to a current figure. The big thing that is wrong with accounting is that it is out of date. Anything we can do to make it more up-to-date — to make it a more realistic picture of the economic world we live in — we ought to do."

Some questions were nevertheless raised about the feasibility of making price level adjustments.

"I question the certainty with which the statement is made concerning the objectivity of adjustments for change in the general price level. . . . The available indices will not remove all distortions and do not take technological improvements into consideration."

"There is a problem of what happens when you adjust fixed assets upwards using general price level indexes in those cases where the new adjusted higher price may be substantially in excess of its economic value."

"What of situations in which replacements in the form of modern equipment (not in kind but serving the same function) are in the offing at costs equal to or below those of present assets, although since the latter's acquisition price levels have increased substantially?"

(2) *Would general price-level adjustments improve the usefulness of financial statements?*

It was asserted that among the most fundamental concepts upon which accounting rests is the distinction between capital and income. Accordingly, it is incumbent upon accountants to strive to do the most effective job possible of recognizing this distinction. It was further argued that improvements in making this distinction might well be in the public interest, as well as in the interest of investors, for in isolating and identifying the effects of inflation the need for dampening further inflationary trends might be dramatized. To some, capital connotes purchasing power; there can be no real income in the absence of an increase in purchasing power. To these people, it follows that, because depreciation tends to be understated in terms of today's dollars, some of today's reported earnings are really a return of capital.

"The basic problem is whether accounting is doing the best job it can do in distinguishing between capital and income. I don't believe the historical statements do as full a job as they would if price level adjustments were made on the basis of the most dependable index that we can have."

"Results of a survey of existing investment literature plus interviews with fifty-one security analysts in New York and Chicago and the scrutiny of 123 of their written analytical reports were reported in the October, 1955, *Accounting Review*:[5] 'When one considers the abundance of literature which has been produced in recent years concerning the impact of changing price levels, the most startling discovery in this investigation has been the united stand of security analysts against 'tampering' with conventional financial statements by applications of price-level adjustments. Not *one* analyst who was interviewed attempts to adjust statements for price level changes. On the contrary, analysts seem to *think* in terms of current dollars. The probable influence of the changing purchasing power of a 1938 dollar and a 1954 dollar is not considered to be relevant in analyzing specific financial data. The general attitude toward formal price level adjustments was succinctly summarized by one prominent analyst who stated, 'Price level? Oh, I suppose we plus and minus mentally for it.' "

"There was a subsequent study conducted by the technical services department of the American Institute of Certified Public Accountants. A questionnaire was sent out to a number of corporate executives in various industries including 'finance and insurance' as one classification. Eighty per cent of that group replied that they would favor a price-level adjustment of depreciation, twenty per cent in that category said they would not favor it. . . . The majority figure in most categories was three to one. . . . It was definitely not connected with taxes because if you connect this thing with taxes there will be complete agreement."

---

[5] Charles T. Horngren, "Security Analysts and the Price Level," *The Accounting Review,* Vol. XXX (October 1955), p. 577.

"We want to measure capital and income. I think that is important, not only to investors but also to the public. Such statements, if they are available, might tend to be a brake on the further 'clippings of the coin' and therefore might affect the public interest."

It was suggested that the responsibility of management for invested capital may well be viewed from the liability side of the balance sheet. For example, the exchange of shares of stock between two individuals does not affect the balance sheet and is of little or no consequence to management; management's responsibility arises when funds are surrendered to the corporation itself. The asset side of the balance sheet shows what has been done with the invested funds made available to management. According to those favoring price level adjustments, a complete job of reporting management's disposition of capital is not accomplished if no distinction is made among dollars of different size. It was argued that dollars of different size must be adjusted for changes in their purchasing power since the date of investment, if financial statements are to be constructed that will report management's responsibility and performance in meaningful terms.

"The responsibility of management is to deal with the capital that has been turned over to them in terms of purchasing power."

"When a person makes an investment in a company, as far as capital is concerned, management should be charged with the preservation of the original investment. . . . The investment is made in cash dollars at the first step. Those dollars could have been used by the person making the investment for any purpose whatsoever. It is the general purchasing power that he is investing in the enterprise. This is what management is charged with preserving for him."

(3) *Are available indexes acceptable?*

Two indexes that might be acceptable are currently available: the Gross National Product Implicit Price Deflator, prepared by the Office of Business Economics of the U.S. Department of Commerce, and the Consumer Price Index, prepared by the Bureau of Labor Statistics of the U.S. Department of Labor. The latter index is perhaps more widely known and understood and might be favored for that reason; however, its effectiveness in measuring what it is designed to measure has received some unfavorable criticism. The former index is based on all transactions entering gross national product statistics, and it therefore represents a broader average. It is undoubtedly less familiar to the average investor, but it is probably less vulnerable to the kind of criticism that is aimed at the Consumer Price Index.

> "The movements of the GNP Implicit Price Deflator and the CPI are much the same. Criticisms of their accuracy or applicability can't change the fact that both indexes reflect a considerable amount of inflation. Of course, my personal view is that even an imperfect index is better than none at all."

Whether a change in the general purchasing power of the dollars invested in a corporation is pertinent to the users of financial statements was questioned by some. General price level indexes measure average purchasing power; whereas, it was argued, individuals are interested primarily in their own specific purchasing power. The number of alternative uses for his funds that an investor is likely to consider are limited. There is no reason to suppose that the prices of the limited alternatives of interest to a particular investor necessarily move in the same direction and in the same magnitude as a general price level index. Such an index is designed to measure the average purchasing power of all individuals based on all kinds of transactions. For that reason, it was suggested, its application may not be relevant for the individual investor.

> "I fail to see how you add to comparability if you are using price indexes which do not apply to the specific industry or the specific company you are dealing with. We know what you can get into when you start dealing with averages."

(4) *Should financial reporting on a price-level adjusted basis be mandatory?*

There has been considerable discussion of the price-level problem in accounting for a number of years. Statements urging experimentation with supplementary information on a voluntary basis have been issued by several influential groups and many prominent individuals. But, except for several case studies undertaken by academicians, and fragmentary applications by a handful of industrial companies, such encouragement has not had any results. This failure is viewed by some as an indication of the lack of need for price-level adjustments.

There is understandable reluctance to require a form of financial reporting the usefulness of which has not been fully tested. On the other hand, some argue that reliance on voluntary experimentation is tantamount to no change. There is a natural reluctance to adopt voluntarily a procedure that tends to reduce reported earnings. A firm competing with other firms in the capital markets may not be in a position to volunteer less favorable financial reports of operations if there is no assurance that competitors will do likewise. Similarly, a firm's management may well be apprehensive about issuing recapitulations of past periods' earnings in the form of five-year or ten-year summaries that contradict previously reported data on earnings. For these reasons, some argue that to suggest that supplementary statements reflecting adjustments for general price level changes be made available on a voluntary basis is likely to be ineffective.

"A lot of people have said that business is not serious about this problem or they would have issued the supplementary statements that the American Institute provides for. But no one in his right mind, with a stock listed on one of the exchanges is going to put out a supplementary statement as long as his competitors and the people he is competing with for capital don't do the same thing. It would be a very quick way of committing financial suicide."

"I disagree that reliance on voluntary experimentation is tantamount to no change, for I fail to see how mandatory requirements add to change in light of the general acceptability concept which has successfully prevailed for a good number of years."

"I think it is important that the accounting profession does not attempt unilaterally to cram this down the throat of the business and financial community. . . . I want to have a good deal more ground-swell and support from the community before I would want to actively push price-level adjustments. I would like to see it done — I would vote that it be done —but I would need a number of people joined on the project."

(5) *Is there a need for price-level adjusted statements under present conditions?*

Some say the moderate degree to which general price levels have changed during recent years tends to diminish their enthusiasm for adjustments. Others point out that some companies have property, plant, and equipment that they acquired years ago. The latter group argue that, even in the absence of future fluctuations in the general price level, there may be a need for such companies to make adjustments to reflect past price-level changes if their reported earnings are not to include a return of capital.

> "I do not agree that many companies have property, plant, and equipment which was acquired years ago. Because of rapid changes in production devices and methods since World War II, a large part of the fixed assets of the average manufacturing business has been recently acquired, and actual costs differ little from replacement costs."

It was also suggested that transition to price-level adjusted financial statements during a relatively stable period is likely to be more orderly and have less drastic short-run effects than under conditions of urgent need. If accounting is to be equipped with an effective tool when the need is critical, ideally that tool should be utilized and perfected in advance.

> "If we postulate an inflation at some point in the future or a significant deflation, unless we have the mechanism well in hand and well-oiled and in being, we are never going to measure that next change."

> "I agree that any tool, to be effective, should be utilized and perfected in advance. However, I believe it should also be stated that we need a reliable index, which we do not have, and an indication of need and importance by users, which we also do not have, before efforts in this direction are undertaken."

It was pointed out that while in the late 1940's the rate of inflation was quite marked, in more recent years the degree of inflation has been quite moderate. And, although the general purchasing power of the dollar has unquestionably declined during the past twenty years, as far as plant and equipment are concerned, improved technology may have operated as a significant offsetting factor. That is, although it may take more dollars today to buy a similar machine, today's machine probably represents greater capacity (e.g., faster, less labor, better quality, etc.). If so, the presumed need for accounting adjustments may be substantially mitigated.

> "I don't believe we can say that the degree of inflation has been 'quite moderate.' As measured by the CPI, there has been an inflation of more than 26% since 1950, and more than 11% since 1955. Furthermore, according to the McGraw-Hill survey of April, 1962, about 40% of all industry's existing plant and equipment was acquired before 1951 and 24% before 1946."

> "What is more disturbing is the expression of the concept that if technology improves enough, accountants can disregard the changes in purchasing power. The two are quite separate. Improvements in technology tend to reduce inflation. In some industries there has been tremendous improvement in technology with consequent actual price reductions, while in other industries there has been little technological improvement and prices have soared. On the average, there has been much improvement in technology but, also on the average, there has been a real inflation. But accountants, of all people, shouldn't be looking at averages, they should be looking at the ranges that go to make up the averages."

(6) *Would price-level adjusted statements be meaningful to users of financial information?*

Some suggest that, in analyzing financial statements, users inherently take into account the fact that there has been an inflationary period. Others caution that adjustments that deal explicitly with inflation might be useful eventually, but considerable educational effort probably would be required before the nature of the adjustments and what they are intended to accomplish were generally understood.

> "It would give improved comparability between companies to have this additional information before the sophisticated investor."

> "I have a lot of trouble with the notion that there would be better comparability between financial statements of the same company or competing companies if price level adjustments were made. I don't think so. There are 101 different reasons why one set of statements differs from another, even in the same company. The causes are various, diffuse, and manifold. Change due to differences in price levels is only one."

Even assuming that the effects of price level changes represent useful information to stockholders, some feel that such information could be provided more effectively in narrative form rather than in the form of supplementary or coordinate financial statements. According to this view, the presentation of two sets of financial statements, each prepared on a different basis, would confuse the reader rather than enlighten him. Others warn that narrative statements are not likely to be disseminated by financial publishers, and such services are an important source of information to investors.

> "There are twenty times as many people who look up a company in the services as there are who look up a company's annual report. . . . The services do not, and presumably will not, carry the president's letter or anything similar, so you are not informing those that you are trying to reach by a narrative."

It also was argued that accounting is primarily concerned with financial statements; accountants are concerned with the information contained in those statements. To suggest that information concerning the effect of price level changes can be handled more effectively in narrative form is to suggest that accounting procedures are inadequate to deal with this problem.

> "You are selling accounting short, if you feel that narrative statements are more informative — more likely to be relied on — than are conventional tabular forms."

> "I doubt that by handling such information in narrative form we even remotely suggest inadequacies in accounting procedures. Unless or until the usefulness of price level information is clearly determined, narrative references to it reflect in no way on existing accounting procedures."

VI | Market Value

The discussions summarized under the heading of market value were concerned with the particular conditions under which the use of market value might be preferred to other bases of valuation and, in addition, the situation in which market value is clearly inappropriate.

Summary of Round Table Discussion

A proposal was made along the following lines: When an asset is acquired initially, it is recorded at cost because that is an expression of the economic value of the service potential in that asset. Subsequent to acquisition, an expression of economic value of the service potential in the asset should continue to be the goal. This would be difficult for the holder to measure, but others may be providing a measurement in terms of prices they are willing to pay for such assets. That is, subsequent to acquisition, market values, to the extent that they are available, should be substituted for cost figures.

The proposal continued: for nonstandardized equipment or equipment that cannot be moved physically, the notion of market value probably has little application. If such equipment continues to be held and utilized, cost is probably the best figure to use. To the extent that obsolescence can be determined, however, it should be recognized. Indeed, obsolescence should be recognized whatever the basis of valuation.

The effect of this proposal, therefore, is the use of market value when obtainable and the use of historical cost whenever market values are not obtainable, with reduction in historical cost to reflect determinable, partial obsolescence.

(1) *Would the use of market values in financial statements be objective?*

It is reasonable to expect that implementation of this proposal would result in sacrifice of some objectivity and feasibility in order to obtain the more useful, or relevant, information that proponents of the use of market values believe such values provide. But the value of property, plant, and equipment is useful information which, in the eyes of proponents, is worth some sacrifice.

> "I am all for original cost, but I do think that there are cases where market value is readily determinable by objective means. Where that is the case, it should be at least footnoted, if not incorporated in the primary statements."

> "I don't know what lack of objectivity can be permitted in a footnote rather than in the statements, but I am as sceptical about putting it in a footnote as I am about substituting it for the historical figure."

To some, the objectivity with which this proposal could be implemented is in doubt. The opportunities for manipulation of financial information may be so great that the proposal must be rejected on that basis alone.

> "This is like a nightmare. . . . I can see management sitting around the table saying, 'What do you think we should make our income this year to maximize the price of our stock? We have been saving these three assets that we know are below market value. Shall we write them up this year, or shall we wait until next year?"

> "It seems to me that the chances for manipulation are so great that you could not consider it on that basis alone."

The use of market values and the recognition of reduced service potential tend to rely in large part on an assessment of the future. It was argued that neither an accountant nor anyone else is equipped to assess the future and that financial statements should be constructed on the basis of past events rather than future expectations. This argument emphasizes a sharp delineation between conventional historical cost accounting and any proposal that calls for "forward accounting." An accounting based on future expectations is said to be vulnerable.

> "If accountants go out on a limb and do something else in making statements other than those based on historical cost, they are getting to a point where they are speculating about an unknown future. I'm very much concerned about the unknown future for the reason that I have seen so many cases where unexpected events have happened in the future that cannot be controlled by the present. In fact, they are completely unknown and unpredictable at the present time. At least you have something to fall back on if you are depending upon historical cost and ordinary depreciation rates on historical cost. You do not have those same things to fall back on — you have only confusion in the picture — when you find that your estimates of what is going to be done in the future were subject to some very foggy notions of decisions that were to be made in the future."

In answer, it has been suggested, however, that even in the conventional balance sheet every item involves an estimate of the future. The value of accounts receivable depends upon their future collectibility; the value of inventories depends upon their future saleability at some minimum price; depreciated historical costs depend upon estimated useful lives. All accounting is largely dependent upon the future.

> "Because we are not quite sure whether the figure ought to be fourteen or fifteen million, we will keep four million on our books. It seems to me that something is wrong. I can't believe that accounting is discharging its obligations when we do this sort of thing. Because we can't be certain of the precise amount of the adjustment, we make none."
>
> ———————

> "I am disturbed to have this described as an innovation in asking us to look to the future. All accounting looks to the future on this sort of thing."

(2) Would the use of market values improve the usefulness of financial statements?

The reporting of assets in financial statements is intended to do two things: (a) to show the resources that have been entrusted to management and for which it is responsible and (b) to show the amount of resources that are going to be deducted from revenues of future periods to determine income. Market value advocates argue that it is important to represent management's responsibility with as current a valuation as possible and to disclose the current economic significance of future benefits as reflected in market prices.

This view is asserted as a logical extension of the use of cost at date of acquisition. Acquisition cost of an asset is presumed to represent valuation of the future benefits which at the time of acquisition are believed to be associated with that asset. The purchaser may have been willing to pay more; competitive forces may have operated in such a way that it was possible to buy for less than the purchaser would have been willing to pay. However, it is not feasible to determine the existence and amount of any such differential. The acquisition cost is accepted as a measure of at least the minimum present value of future benefits.

For pieces of equipment that are separable, mobile, and standardized, management must continually weigh the advantages of continued use in its operations or disposal at its market price. Current market value, it is asserted, continues to indicate the minimum value to the firm; its value to the firm must be assumed to be at least that great, or the equipment would be sold.

It is argued that if a fundamental change from the traditional accounting for historical acquisition costs is to be undertaken — a change that may involve a painful and costly transition and one that may require a re-education process for investors and other users of financial statements — the change should be toward presentation of the kind of information that is really significant. In the eyes of advocates of use of market value, the significant information is information about value, about management's responsibility, about the economic sacrifice of depreciating assets, and about the economic sacrifice that has been made in the production of revenue.

> "I don't know how much general applicability it can command, but it spells out two things we want to know from our financial statement: What is it that management is responsible for and what economic resources are sacrificed in the production of revenues?"

> ———

> "The proposal sounds like a conglomeration of as many valuation bases as possible. I can imagine the confusion of the users of financial statements if they were presented with such a basis for asset valuation."

> ———

"I don't think the investor is interested in the value of a plant in a going concern. I don't think management has any responsibility to maintain the value of a plant in a going concern. The investor is interested in total value. He is interested in the intangibles. If management has any responsibility, it is responsible to maintain total value. . . . I don't say the current balance sheet shows value but this balance sheet wouldn't show value either."

"Whether we take the market price or whether we take adjusted values of any kind other than historical cost, what we are missing are future decisions. We don't know what the decisions are going to be tomorrow with respect to a certain asset."

(3) *To what extent would the use of market values in financial statements be feasible?*

Advocates recognize that there are a great many items of plant and equipment for which reliable estimates of market value are not obtainable. In the case of land, market values are likely to be determinable, but the need is less acute, inasmuch as charges against future revenues are not involved. For those items of plant and equipment for which reliable market values are not available, in the absence of convincing evidence that the original estimates of service potential were not clearly overstated or understated, probably the best measurement that can be provided is depreciated cost.

"This must be a very limited per cent of the total assets in American industry that we are talking about. It must be a fraction of one per cent."

"I like market. I disagree with that one per cent. If industry would look around they would discover a surprising number of things for which an accurate market value could be determined."

(4) *What method of valuation should be used when market values are unobtainable or inappropriate?*

Where there is substantial technological progress, it may be clear that the original estimates of service potential were wrong. This does not necessarily mean, however, that management will dispose of used plant and equipment in favor of new technologically advanced plant and equipment. Continued possession and use of the old equipment may still be economically justified although its value may be significantly diminished. That is, service potential may be eroded without necessarily being eliminated by obsolescence. Some assert that in such cases depreciated cost should be reduced. It was suggested that in many cases management's analysis of the economic merits of replacement of the old with the new will be available and can be used as the basis for determining an appropriate reduction.

Unforeseen reductions in service potential may also occur in the absence of technological advances, as in the case of shifts in demand for a firm's product. Under these circumstances, depreciated cost may overstate the value of service potential. In these cases, unfortunately, management is not likely to have undertaken an economic analysis that would suggest an appropriate reduction.

> "The most dramatic example of obsolescence at the moment is the open hearth blast furnace. If they are compared with how you would do if you had an oxygen process, a very substantial write-down is presently called for. The precise amount would almost certainly be wrong. The question is, would it be more wrong than the figures now on the books?"

> "I would use your approach as a suggestion that depreciation policies ought to be reviewed care-

fully — more carefully than normal — at least once every five or six years — to see whether a fair representation is being made of the proper amount of cost deferable to the future."

That part of the proposal involving the write-down of plant and equipment in recognition of unforeseen obsolescence may be consistent with current accounting practice. Some feel that if it were to become automatic, however, the opportunities for manipulation might be increased, and adequate verification might be difficult. Some would consider it unrealistic or even misleading if the proposed write-down permitted a firm whose plant and equipment were relatively obsolete to report a rate of return that was as good as, or better than, that of a firm operating a modern, efficient plant. The contrary argument says that if, rather than abandoning it, management made a correct economic decision to retain and utilize a relatively obsolete plant because it had positive revenue potential, financial statements should reflect this correct decision favorably. If obsolescence is not recognized when it is clearly evident, costs will continue to be based on the unreduced book value, and management's correct decision to retain and use may be reflected unfavorably in the financial reports.

> "Take the example of the open hearth furnace and the oxygen processing plant. Assume you can make the adjustment accurately. The write-down of the open hearth furnace is made in such a way that the stream of future economic benefits, together with the operating costs, will perhaps produce a result comparable with those companies using the oxygen processing method. Obviously, they are not in a comparable position. . . . Open hearth companies now have a small investment and therefore are producing a higher rate of return. I think this is misleading."

VII | Replacement Cost

Summary of Round Table Discussion

(1) *Would the use of replacement costs enhance the usefulness of financial statements?*

As is true with all methods of asset valuation, the case for the use of replacement costs depends on the concept of income that accounting is attempting to measure. One concept is based on the premise that the measurement of income is relevant to the investor as an indication of dividend paying potential. Although the payment of dividends is subject to certain legal restrictions, it is argued that there are very few corporations whose dividend policy actually is affected by those restrictions. According to this view, in the vast majority of cases, dividend policy is established as a matter of managerial decision, which may be influenced by a variety of external pressures more influential than legal provisions.

Some believe that management is not likely to declare dividends that would, in effect, diminish productive capacity. It is argued that managements are physically oriented as well as value oriented — perhaps physically oriented to a greater extent. Some claim that there is evidence that the funds required to replace capacity must be internally generated. It is argued that managements of American corporations tend to be reluctant to go out into the capital market for funds needed to continue existing capacity — indeed, they seem to be reluctant currently to raise funds in the capital market for expansion. This being the case, it is said, investors may not reasonably anticipate dividends unless internally generated funds are at least adequate for replacement of capacity. In terms of usefulness to investors, therefore, advocates conclude that depreciation should be based on the replacement cost of plant and equipment. Admittedly, this will not necessarily provide the precise figures of primary interest to investors — dividends may not be declared even in the face of adequate internally generated funds — but, it is argued, the resultant income measurement would be considerably more useful than that now obtained on the basis of historical cost.

> "When I started in business, net earnings meant net earnings for the payment of dividends — period! It is a damn shame how far away from that we have gotten."

> "This will not give us what I would say is the figure that the stockholder is really interested in, but it moves us closer to it than historical cost does."

In support of the use of replacement costs, J. R. Hicks' well-known concept of income was cited. Crudely stated, his definition of income was the amount that a company could spend and still be as "well off as before." It was suggested that the major difference between proposals to use market value and proposals to use replacement cost is the measure of "well-offness." The former is concerned with value; the latter is concerned with productive capacity. Those who favor the use of replacement cost argue that the most useful measure of depreciation is one that represents the expired services that must be replaced in order to perpetuate the current level of earning power.

> "I have seen some real weird conclusions reached

from crude statements of Hicks' concept, and I think we would be well advised not to rely on any such statement."

It was pointed out that whether management will declare dividends in the future is necessarily uncertain, and an income figure dependent upon possible future management actions may be misleading. On the other hand, proponents argue that the only way in which future considerations can be completely eliminated in accounting is to report only cash receipts and cash disbursements. Any measurement of income involving depreciation is based on uncertainty.

"The minimum amount of internally generated funds that management is going to retain is the amount that will be necessary to maintain capacity. Now I think they are going to retain more than that because it is probable that they are going to want to grow at least as fast as the industry has grown, so there is going to be a further drain that the stockholder will never get in a payment. We are not measuring perfection. This is not an ideal. This is just a quarter of a step away from historical cost and not much more than that."

"Indicating, even by way of comment, what the division of either income or surplus might be . . . would be an extremely misleading figure because we don't know what decision is going to be made in the future."

"If we are going to take the position that we can't account because we don't know the decisions that management is going to make in the future, then we can't set up any deduction for depreciation at all, except either at the time that the property is purchased or when it is sold."

(2) *Would the use of replacement costs in financial statements be objective and feasible?*

Objectivity and feasibility are major problems in connection with this proposal. It is argued that available indexes that might be applied to historical cost in order to approximate replacement cost can by no means produce accurate results. On the other hand, proponents argue that it is feasible to apply them with complete objectivity and if the results were more useful — in that they would more closely fulfill investors' needs — the lack of complete accuracy should not preclude their use.

> "I am inclined to think that the indexes that measure replacement cost are not accurate or anywhere near accurate, but I think they are objective and that the use of these indexes would move us a little bit closer — how much closer, we don't have the slightest idea — a little bit closer to giving an income figure that the stockholders want."

(3) *Could the use of specific price indexes provide acceptable approximations of current replacement cost?*

The inaccuracies involved in the application of most replacement cost indexes to specific assets are probably among the most significant obstacles to a favorable attitude toward their use.

It is argued that replacement cost indexes do not include an accurate allowance for technological change. For example, although equipment may be replaced at a price greater than historical cost, it may be more efficient equipment — it may reduce the amount of labor required — and depreciation based on replacement cost may be excessive in terms of maintenance of dividend paying capacity.

> "Maybe the machine costs more now, but it is much more efficient economically, and the index of replacement cost does not take this into considera-

tion. Therefore, if you depreciate purely on the basis of replacement cost, you would be excessively depreciating."

"I don't believe we know whether or not replacement cost indexes can include an accurate allowance for technological change. If they cannot, then how can the Consumers Price Index do this? The Consumers Price Index includes prices of housing, of drugs, of automobiles, of hard household goods. Hasn't there been technological change in all of these? The same problem is involved in the GNP Implicit Price Deflator. Capital goods are in there. If it cannot be done, then it can't be done for the GNP index. Why are we chasing the will-of-the-wisp of accuracy?"

"In certain specific situations fairly accurate indexes can be and have been devised. I don't believe, however, that accuracy is the most significant obstacle to a favorable attitude toward their use. I think that a greater obstacle is that replacement does not fit basic accounting concepts."

Some assert that there is reason to believe that management will not declare dividends until there are sufficient internally generated funds to replace its plant and equipment, even though the new plant and equipment are a great deal more efficient. Acording to this view, management tends to be volume oriented; it is unthinkable to management to allow productive capacity to be diminished.

"What reasons do we have for believing this? I have seen very close correlations between the movement of the CPI and the increase in retained earnings of some of the larger corporations, even though replacement costs were increasing much faster. I believe the fact is that many managements have not been able to prevent a diminution in productive capacity, particularly where long-lived plant is involved."

VIII | Some Personal Observations of the Moderator and the Reporter

For reasons given earlier, the members of the Round Table agreed not to attempt to reach a consensus or to formulate a set of over-all conclusions. Nevertheless, it seems appropriate that the Moderator and the Reporter make some personal observations growing out of the Round Table discussions. We did not participate in the exchange of opinions; our roles were those of Moderator and Reporter, in the literal meaning of these words.

The purpose of the Round Table was to identify the issues and the arguments relating to the accounting for property, plant, and equipment so that further discussion and resolution would be facilitated. We think this purpose was accomplished in three very important respects.

First, we think that the definition of the problem as set forth in Chapter II and the criteria against which proposals were tested as described in Chapter III will be useful to other groups who discuss the problem. The half day spent discussing this definition and these criteria could have been frustrating, since the participants were eager to get to the issue itself, but it was not. Instead, the definition and criteria turned out to be extremely useful in keeping the remainder of the discussion focused.

We suggest that other groups will find this approach equally useful. If the participants can agree at the outset on statements substantially like those described in

Chapters II and III, they can proceed even more quickly than we did to the heart of the discussion. Even if they do not agree exactly with our definitions and criteria, time spent in reaching explicit agreement on some alternative is likely to be worthwhile.

Each of the eight points listed in Chapter II has a purpose; the omission of any one of them would have led to difficulties in the subsequent discussion. Some of these points excluded important but separable problems, such as the treatment of long-term leases, donated assets, and wasting assets. The central issue is big enough by itself, without an attempt to reach agreement on these related questions. The statement of the problem also kept us focused on the point of view of the informed investor. Other points of view are relevant: those of the general public (described as "the little old lady from Keokuk problem"), income tax regulations, special interests of commercial banks, attitude of labor unions, and so on. Nevertheless, restricting the discussion to the investor's viewpoint prevented a considerable amount of diffusion, which often takes place in such discussions.

The second accomplishment of the Round Table, we believe, is that it singled out those alternatives that were worth serious consideration. As Appendix B indicates, eight possible solutions were submitted for consideration by the Round Table. Some of these were dismissed in their entirety, and certain aspects of others quite obviously had no support among the participants, and we think it is a reasonable inference that there is little support for them in any segment of the business community. Those rejected are as follows:

(a) *Economic value*, or more precisely, the present value of the future earning power of the assets. There was a complete absence of support for such a method of valuation for the foreseeable future. Moreover, there also was strong (although not unanimous) sentiment that it was not worthwhile to bring this possibility into the discussion even as some "ideal" or "distant goal" against which other alternatives should be tested. Discussion of this alternative got nowhere.

(b) *Appraisal value.* Although some interest was expressed initially in the possibility of basing the measurement on appraisal value, this interest evaporated after the practical problems of implementing a system of appraisals as the normal basis for balance sheet reporting were thoroughly aired. The appraisal process involves a considerable amount of judgment, and it is inconceivable that the appraisal profession could be expanded sufficiently to insure competent appraisals of all business property on a routine basis. An alternative would be to develop a set of formulas, including an index number series for each category of assets, that would approximate the way in which appraisers arrive at their judgments and would be used directly by businesses to determine asset values. It seemed generally agreed that such a method would not be feasible.

(c) *Market value,* without stringent qualification. Although there was some interest in use of market value, those who advocated this had a highly circumscribed notion of market value. There was no support for the idea of using it as the routine basis for balance sheet reporting of most fixed asset items. Those who support its use do so only when there is reliable evidence as to the market value of the specific asset involved. This situation was believed to apply to such a small fraction of the total stock of fixed assets that the approach might better be thought of as an occasional exception to the cost basis, rather than a fundamental departure from it.

Finally, we think the discussion brought out most of the significant questions relating to the remaining alternatives, as far as they can be brought out on any logical basis. In other words, from here on, the resolution of the issue depends on how practical men weigh the importance of the various factors that have been brought out. It is unlikely that many, if any, new factors will enter into the discussion.

Without significant oversimplification, we think it can be said that the alternatives worth serious discussion are represented by three groups:

(a) There are those who believe that no change in or supplement to the historical cost method would bring benefits equal to the cost and risk involved — the cost of implementation and the risk of misinterpretation. Some advocates of historical cost will continue to hold to this view unless they are given convincing evidence that an alternative will produce markedly more useful results.

(b) Closely allied, are those who wish to preserve historical cost as the primary basis for financial statements but who advocate the simultaneous and complimentary presentation of financial statements that have been adjusted for changes in the general price level. These advocates believe that management has a fiduciary accountability in terms of current purchasing power in addition to an accountability for historical dollars. None of this group favors elimination of historical cost in the foreseeable future, although some might favor elimination subsequently, if the adjusted statements prove to be as useful as expected.

(c) Others believe that acquisition cost should be modified under certain carefully defined circumstances to recognize changes in the price of specific assets, as indicated either by market value of these assets or by specific price indexes. This group may be further subdivided into those who feel that only a single modification of cost should be made and those who feel that the modification should be divided into two parts — one part reflecting a change in the general price level since acquisition and the other part indicating the difference in movement between the specific price of this asset and that of all prices in general.

The advocates of modifying historical acquisition cost would do so only when there is objective evidence that the current value of an asset differs materially from its book value. The meaning of "objective evidence" has to be carefully spelled out. Essentially, it means that departures above depreciated historical cost are limited to some or all of the following categories: land, in areas where land values are fairly readily measured; oil and mineral reserves and rights with proven value; and depreciable assets, under clearly prescribed circumstances, such as by reference to the current cost of comparable assets, if they are bought and sold in a discernible market, or possibly by reference to specific price indexes when application is deemed valid. Decreases would be recognized whenever assets have unmistakeably become obsolete — a practice generally considered proper by those who favor accounting for historical costs.

Those who advocate a general price level adjustment usually, but not always, justify it in terms of the need for a new unit of measurement — a quantity of purchasing power rather than the legal dollar. This method requires that the adjustment be made to all items on the balance sheet, rather than to fixed assets alone. It is conceptually preferable, therefore, to view the problem of general price level adjustments in a context broader than the measurement of property, plant, and equipment; as a practical matter, however, it is probably impossible to exclude the possibility of general price level adjustments only, in a discussion of the fixed asset problem.

This is as far as we go, and as far as we think we should go at this time. It is as far as we think any unofficial discussion group such as ours can go. The Round Table identified the feasible alternatives and the questions that need to be answered. In our opinion, no chain of logical, mathematical, or economic reasoning will *prove* that one of these alternatives is the best. If a change should be made (and we are not implying that a change is or is not needed), it will be made only as a result of the action of informed, practical people. The decision of these people will reflect their judgment as to which alternative represents the best balance among the criteria of objectivity, feasibility, and usefulness.

Appendix A

Letter of Invitation

HARVARD UNIVERSITY

GRADUATE SCHOOL OF BUSINESS ADMINISTRATION

GEORGE F. BAKER FOUNDATION

OFFICE OF THE DEAN

SOLDIERS FIELD
BOSTON 63, MASSACHUSETTS

Date

Mr. xxxxxx xxxxxxxx
xxxxxxxxxxxxxxxxxxxxxx
xxxxxxxxxxxxxxxxxxxxxx
xxxxxxxxxxxxxxxxxxxxxx

Dear Mr. xxxxxxxx:

We invite you to become a member of an Accounting Principles Round Table which we are organizing for the purpose of discussing in some depth the accounting treatment of fixed assets in published financial statements. As you know, some have proposed that replacement costs or price-level adjusted costs should be used instead of historical costs, and others believe that such proposals are not useful or feasible.

The group will consist of men from industry, the public accounting profession, government, universities, and the financial community, about twelve or fourteen persons in all. The discussion will be entirely private. Hopefully, from an exchange of the various points of view represented, there will emerge a rather specific statement of areas of agreement and disagreement which will be helpful to those who have this problem under consideration. This effort is separate from the activities of the American Institute of Certified Public Accountants, but we are working closely with the AICPA.

We plan to convene the Round Table on Monday and Tuesday, April 29 and 30, in a Conference House in the Boston area. Prior to the meeting we shall collect and furnish such background information as the participants wish to have.

Professor Robert N. Anthony will act as moderator and will be in charge of arrangements. He will be glad to answer questions you have about it (Area 617, KI 7-9800).

We look upon this Round Table as an opportunity to make significant progress in resolving a currently controversial question. We hope you will be willing to participate in it.

Sincerely yours,

George P. Baker
Dean

Advance Document:
Statement of Proposals

It is assumed that among those bases for determining the amount at which plant and equipment should be reported in published financial statements, the Round Table will wish to consider the following. Perhaps certain of these proposals will prove to be unacceptable after only brief consideration and perhaps members of the Round Table will wish to expand the list with other proposals deemed worthy of consideration.

(1) *Historical cost*
(2) *Historical cost or "market," whichever is lower*
(3) *Adjusted cost*
(4) *Historical cost adjusting for* general *price-level changes*
(5) *Economic value*
(6) *Market value*
(7) *Appraisal value*
(8) *Price-index replacement cost*

It is to be noted that these are referred to as *bases* for determining appropriate amounts for disclosure in financial statements. It is assumed that the accumulated depreciation of depreciable assets will be deducted in arriving at the net carrying value. It is common practice to disclose the gross amount (before consideration of any accumulated depreciation) and the amount of any accumulated depreciation as well as the net carrying value. As indicated earlier, it is assumed that all amounts associated with an asset (gross amount, depreciation, accumulated depreciation, and net carrying value) will be consistent with the *basis* selected.

An effort to clarify the concept identified by each of these terms and to indicate some of its attributes follows:

(1) Historical cost

Concept: Paton and Littleton supply a lucid exposition of the concept of historical cost as it is generally held.

> In ideal situations cost is gauged by the amount of cash which is immediately expended to acquire the particular commodity or service involved. For many transactions, however, the payment of cash is delayed for some time and in these cases true cost is measured by the amount of cash that would have to be expended if final settlement were effected at once. . . .
>
> It is hardly necessary to state that when a tangible asset is purchased all costs necessary for acquiring the property and for placing it in position to serve the particular function for which it is intended should be included in the cost of property.[6]

Attributes: Historical costs are presumed to represent objective measurements resulting from arms-length transactions between purchasers and sellers. The cost incurred, therefore, may be assumed to represent the market value of the asset acquired at the time of acquisition. Subsequent adherence to historical cost results in the postponement of recognition of changes in value (other than depreciation) until such changes are "realized" by sale (of the asset itself, or its product) or other disposition. The rationale underlying the use of historical costs has been explained by A. C. Littleton as follows:

> Management is duty bound to invest (buy) enterprise assets at the most advantageous available price and to disinvest (sell) at the most advantageous available price. That is a fundamental part of

---

[6] W. A. Paton and A. C. Littleton, *An Introduction to Corporate Accounting Standards* (American Accounting Association, 1940), pp. 26 and 31.

the working of our system of free enterprise. The system stands to suffer in some degree, and management surely is handicapped, if responsible executives cannot judge in retrospect the outcome of prior commitments. A classified record of transactions stated in terms of invested costs (prior commitments) would seem an essential element for this use.

As a consequence, accounting has an obligation to record and report historical or invested cost, not as a convention or a tradition, but as a service necessity.[7]

(2) HISTORICAL COST OR "MARKET," WHICHEVER IS LOWER

Concept: Essentially, this is the well-known inventory rule applied to property, plant, and equipment. Whenever it becomes evident that current value (e.g., market value or replacement cost) is materially less than the carrying value as determined on the basis of historical cost, the former is adopted. For example, if it becomes apparent that land which was acquired at a cost of $100,000 currently has a market value of only $60,000, the carrying value is reduced to $60,000.

Attributes: This method manifests the widely accepted accounting doctrine of conservatism, that is, the recognition of all losses but the anticipation of no gains. To paraphrase the comments contained in Accounting Research Bulletin 43 concerning "inventory pricing," a departure from the cost basis is required when "utility" is no longer as great as its cost. Where there is evidence that "utility" in the ordinary course of business will be less than cost "whether due to physical deterioration, ob-

---

[7] A. C. Littleton, "Significance of Invested Cost," *The Accounting Review,* April 1952, p. 171.

solescence, changes in price levels, or other courses, the difference should be recognized as a loss of the current period."[8]

According to Carman Blough:

> The convention of anticipating losses but not profits is one of the oldest principles of accounting. It has evolved from, and has been proven desirable by, the experiences of businessmen for generations. Consistency has its place, and in some accounting matters it is of paramount importance, but there are limitations both to its usefulness and to its applicability. Experience has demonstrated that it is sound business policy to wait until profits are realized before they are reported while providing for losses as soon as they are apparent. Too many businesses have gone into bankruptcy for not observing such a principle to warrant brushing it aside merely because it seems *not* to be internally consistent.[9]

William W. Werntz has also suggested that "there is a vast difference between using a price quotation as a means of estimating a loss and using the same quotation as a means of recognizing a profit to be reflected in the accounts. The latter requires a far higher degree of exactness and objectivity than the former." When an appraisal is used "to write down property," there is no objection, "as the appraisal is . . . only a method of estimating a loss." [10]

(3) ADJUSTED COST

Concept: "Adjusted cost" refers to the suggestion that the basis for valuation of property, plant, and equipment

---

[8] AICPA, Committee on Accounting Procedure, *Restatement and Revision of Accounting Research Bulletins,* op. cit. p. 30.

[9] Comments of Carman G. Blough contained in Robert T. Sprouse and Maurice Moonitz, *A Tentative Set of Broad Accounting Principles for Business Enterprises,* Accounting Research Study No. 3 (New York, AICPA, 1962), p. 61.

[10] Comments of William W. Werntz, *ibid.,* p. 81.

be historical cost unless there is objective evidence that market value *exceeds* the amount determined on that basis, in which case the asset should be *written up* to its market value. In effect, this proposal calls for historical cost or "market," whichever is *higher*.

Attributes: This proposal has been made as a compromise for those who favor historical cost and those who favor current value. The adjusted cost approach attempts to take into account the merits of objectivity epitomized by historical cost and the relevance of current value. Most examples cited by current value advocates relate to situations where current value *exceeds* historical cost. Under these circumstances *and* when there is objective evidence to support the figure, the carrying value of the asset should be *adjusted* to current value. Unless both conditions prevail, carrying value continues to be based on historical cost. The effect is that current value governs in those circumstances where its advocates demonstrate it to be the more meaningful figure, but only in those circumstances. In the absence of such evidence, the verifiable historical cost governs.

(4) HISTORICAL COST ADJUSTED FOR
GENERAL PRICE LEVEL CHANGES

Concept: In order to account for the effects of price-level changes in the measurement of income and state each asset in dollars of the same purchasing power, it is necessary to adjust the historical costs of property, plant, and equipment as maintained by conventional accounting methods. The adjustment can be accomplished by the application of some general price-level index such as the Gross National Product Implicit Price Deflator prepared by the Office of Business Economics of the U.S. Department of Commerce and the Consumer Price Index prepared by the Bureau of Labor Statistics of the U.S. Department of Labor.

This concept is not to be confused with proposals to

adjust historical cost records by the application of *specific* price indexes in order to approximate current replacement cost. (The concept of price-index replacement cost is discussed later.) As explained by the American Accounting Association's Committee on Concepts and Standards Underlying Corporate Financial Statements:

> . . . the adjustment of historical dollar costs — the restatement of these costs in current dollars of equivalent purchasing power as measured by a *general* price index — is independent of estimated replacement costs or replacement policy. It differs from the conventional original dollar cost concept only in that it recognizes changes in the value of the dollar and reflects these changes in the amortization of costs and in the determination of periodic income. Its application is independent of possible or probable future price changes, either upward or downward, since only past changes in the value of the dollar are reflected in the adjusted figures.[11]

Attributes: One of the primary objectives of price-level adjustments is to restate accounts in terms of a common measuring unit. In the words of Perry Mason:

> The principal point to keep in mind is that the dollars of different years represent different amounts of commodities and services and that amounts expressed in dollars of various years should not be compared, added, or subtracted unless adjustments are made so that the dollar represents a uniform measure of business activity. . . . A useful analogy can be drawn between price-level adjustments and the conversion of foreign curren-

---

[11] American Accounting Association, Committee on Concepts and Standards Underlying Corporate Financial Statements "Price Level Changes and Financial Statements." Supplementary Statement No. 2, *The Accounting Review*, October 1951, p. 471.

cies. It would not occur to anyone to add amounts stated in pounds, pesos, francs, or even Canadian dollars to amounts stated in United States dollars without first converting the foreign currencies with the use of appropriate exchange rates. Yet we are in the habit of treating dollars of different years as identical even though, like the foreign currencies, they represent different amounts of goods and services and should be converted to a constant-dollar basis in order to make them comparable.[12]

In addition to satisfying a principle of measurement and mathematics — comparative measurements and mathematical operations must be performed in terms of a common denominator — price-level adjustments are intended to produce a more meaningful income figure.

> The effects of inflation, as evidenced by the reducing purchasing power of our unit of financial reporting, the dollar, are not recognized in today's conventional accounting procedures. As a consequence the conventional income statement results in a stated net income which is at variance with, and usually exceeds, true income as recognized by the economists. These facts are too well known to require explanation or discussion.
>
> . . . There has been strong advocacy by accountants of prominence of the necessity for modifying conventional accounting methods to recognize the effect of inflation on depreciation as a major cost factor, and thus produce a reported net income less at variance with true income, but the adoption of such procedures has been rare.[13]

---

[12] Perry Mason, *Price-Level Changes and Financial Statements,* Basic Concepts and Methods (American Accounting Association, 1956), p. 10.

[13] Anson Herrick, "Inflation in Accounting," *Journal of Accountancy,* September 1960, p. 51.

The adjustment for general price-level changes is intended to take into account changes in the dollar as a measuring unit only; it does not take into account changes in the "prices" of individual assets themselves. Whether the "prices" of individual assets change in a magnitude different from the general price level or, indeed, change in a *direction* different from the general price level is not relevant. Adjustments for general price-level changes may be designed to adhere to the notion of "invested cost," but measured in terms of constant purchasing power. Or, such adjustments may be looked upon as one of the steps in accounting for changes both in the general price level and in the prices of specific assets.

Although the round table will focus its attention on accounting for property, plant, and equipment, advocates of general price level adjustments often propose comprehensive adjustments of all financial accounts. The following is representative of the underlying rationale:

> . . . without adjustment of the figures the income statement suffers from price-level changes by the lack of comparability of the accounting figures, from the failure of depreciation and similar costs to reflect the current price level and therefore to be comparable with the current revenue figures, and from the resulting diminished significance of the reported net income. The balance sheet also suffers from lack of comparability of the various items. Cash and receivables and the unpaid liabilities are expressed in current dollars, but the inventories and especially the plant and equipment are collections of noncomparable items since they are almost always a hodge-podge of various past-period dollars representing different amounts of purchasing power over commodities and services.[14]

---

[14] Perry Mason, op. cit., p. 11.

In most of the instances where price-level adjustments have been made in published financial statements, they have been made only with respect to selected accounts. For example, the 1961 annual report of Ayrshire Collieries Corporation includes an adjustment for "price-level depreciation" in the income statement but the assets remain unadjusted. The 1961 annual report of Indiana Telephone Corporation contains adjustments for "variations in the purchasing power of the dollar" in accounting for plant in a supplementary balance sheet as well as in accounting for depreciation in a supplementary income statement. No other adjustments are made. The Accounting Research Division of the AICPA has recently made available a rather exhaustive study of such disclosures, a copy of which is being distributed to each member of the round table.

(5) ECONOMIC VALUE

Concept: The economic value of an asset is the present value of all future returns (cash receipts) which are attributable to its possession and/or use, determined at an appropriate rate of discount and measured in a constant monetary unit. A business enterprise engages in a continuous process of acquiring factors and converting them to cash. The essence of the value of an asset, therefore, is the present value of the future cash receipts (or their equivalent) into which that asset will be converted.

Attributes: This method requires information concerning amount of future cash flows, timing of such cash flows, the applicable discount rate, and relevant price-level changes. With the exception of the last factor, this method is widely employed in the valuation of long-term receivables and payables (e.g., bonds) and sometimes in other situations, usually contractual in nature, where such information is available. Its use is probably not feasible, however, for the valuation of individual assets where their contributions toward future cash flows is inextricably combined with those of other factors. For example, even if the amount and timing of cash flows resulting from the manufacture and sale of a product were known, the portions attributable to each factor of production (materials, labor, facilities, management) cannot be isolated.

(6) MARKET VALUE

Concept: Market value is the price at which an exchange transaction could take place currently, assuming that the asset were to continue in the use for which it is intended. At the time of acquisition, "cost" and "market value" are presumably identical; subsequently, "cost" remains unchanged and becomes historical in nature. However, as a consequence of changing economic conditions, "market value" is apt to diverge from historical cost. "Market value" is intended to imply something distinct from "liquidation value" and "scrap value." As one extreme, in the absence of a "market" for an asset itself, "market value" is assumed to embrace the contribution made by an asset toward the market value of the products or services which may be produced with it. Often, however, the use of market value is advocated only for those assets for which a "market" exists (e.g., among fixed assets, for most land, some buildings, general-purpose machinery and equipment, etc.) and for which, therefore, "market value" determinations may be feasible.

Attributes: James L. Dohr, while Director of Research for the then American Institute of Accountants wrote:

> The financial significance of property is manifestly to be determined largely from present facts and prospects rather than from past facts; the latter are ordinarily of importance only so far as they may be said to indicate what is likely to happen in the future. As a result the *present value* of property is, generally speaking, the factor of outstanding importance; it indicates, with varying degrees

of accuracy, what the owner may expect to realize upon a sale; it determines his borrowing capacity insofar as the property is concerned; it fixes his liability for various forms of taxation; it reflects his earning capacity as owner; it may be said to measure his ability to make gifts; it is the basis upon which the property may be insured.[15]

Dohr concluded that:

> . . . the significance of items of property at any given time is frequently determined by present or market value. Manifestly, present value cannot be ignored entirely, or even relegated to footnote comment, if accounting is to be of a maximum usefulness to the various interested parties. As a matter of fact, as time goes on and business enterprises change hands, or as businesses are reorganized under various statutes, there is a continuous process or restatement in terms of present values.[16]

Dohr recommended that whenever present value is greatly below cost or greatly in excess of cost and the evidence indicates clearly that the disparity is likely to prevail for some time, appropriate recognition be given to fairly determined present value.[17]

The use of market value is widespread for those assets for which an established market exists and quotations are readily obtainable, e.g., for the marketable securities held by investment trusts, for certain agricultural products, and for certain basic metals and other extractive products. It has rarely been adopted for property, plant, and equipment.

The use of market value is not solely a balance sheet

[15] James L. Dohr, "Cost and Value," *Journal of Accountancy*, March 1944, p. 193.

[16] *Ibid.*, pp. 195-196.

[17] *Ibid.*, p. 196.

consideration; it has significant implications for the determination of income. Indeed, its advocates often emphasize the latter. In the case of property, plant, and equipment for which market values exist, presumably management is continually considering the alternative advantages of continued use or disposal. Hence, in the measurement of income it may be said that the "cost" of continued use is the sacrifice of alternative proceeds. It is argued that the failure to recognize market values tends to distort the measurement of income in this sense; the user is unable to evaluate management's ability to analyze the alternatives and select that which is most economically advantageous.

(7) Appraisal value

Concept: Appraisal value refers to the results of systematic professional analysis of "property facts, rights, investments, and values, based primarily on a personal inspection and inventory of the property"[18] and presumably conducted by an independent expert. The results would ordinarily be expressed in terms of reproduction cost less accumulated depreciation although, for certain types of property, plant, and equipment (e.g., land), current market values represent a *major* consideration.

Currently, the use of appraisal values is apparently embraced by "generally accepted accounting principles." Accounting Research Bulletin 5, issued in April 1940, contained the statement that "Accounting for fixed assets should normally be based on cost, and any attempt to make property accounts in general reflect current values is both impractical and inexpedient. Appreciation normally should not be reflected on the books of account of corporations." Nevertheless, the bulletin went on to

---

[18] Association of Appraisal Executives, *Basic Standards of Appraisal Practice and Procedure* (Washington, D.C., Association of Appraisal Executives, 1936), p. 10.

make recommendations "where appreciation has in fact been entered on the books."[19]

In Accounting Research Bulletin 43, issued in 1953, a different attitude is reflected: "Historically, fixed assets have been accounted for on the basis of cost. However, fixed assets in the past have occasionally been written up to appraised values because of rapid rises in price levels, to adjust costs in the case of bargain purchases, etc."[20] The practice is not criticized.

The "opinion of independent public accountants" presented in the 1961 annual report of Creole Petroleum Corporation contains the following statements:

> An independent appraisal was made of the company's investment in physical plant, and the amount of such appraisal over unamortized cost, amounting to $405,955,005, was added to net Property, Plant and Equipment. . . . Under generally accepted accounting principles such revaluations, although seldom now adopted by companies in the United States for statement purposes, are generally regarded as permissible where appraised current values are formally recorded for all productive facilities subject to depreciation.[21]

Attributes: It is argued that when carrying values based on historical costs are significantly different from current values as determined by appraisal, the balance sheet no longer represents a useful statement of financial position — the disclosure of "historical costs not yet amortized" has no economic significance. In advocating the use of appraisal values, however, major emphasis is

---

[19] AICPA, Committee on Accounting Procedure, *Depreciation on Appreciation,* Accounting Research Bulletin No. 5 (New York, AICPA, 1940), p. 37.

[20] AICPA, Committee on Accounting Procedure, *Restatement and Revision of Accounting Research Bulletins,* op. cit., p. 73.

[21] *Annual Report 1961,* Creole Petroleum Corporation, p. 28.

usually placed upon the measurement of income. The President of Creole Petroleum Corporation, for example, explained:

> For some time, it had been increasily apparent that the unamortized portion of the company's investments in physical plant, as recorded on its books based on historical costs, failed to reflect the true value of such investments when compared with today's much higher costs for the labor, material and services required in drilling and construction. This condition caused depreciation to be understated in terms of present costs and at the same time reflected earnings as being disproportionately high in relation to net assets.[22]

Presumably income represents the amount which could be distributed in the form of dividends without contracting the economic resources of the enterprise, or, in the absence of dividends, the amount of additional resources available for expansion and growth. The single most widely-used financial statistic, earnings-per-share, and its use in relationship to the current quotation of market price per share is a manifestation of this attitude. To the extent that deductions made in the measurement of income misstate the cost of maintaining (replacing) the resources exhausted in that period's operations, it is difficult to interpret the results of operations. That is, reported net income represents something more or less than the amount that can be used for dividends or growth. If current costs are higher than historical costs, some reported income must be retained merely to maintain existing resources, and, if the exhausted resources can be replaced at a cost less than historical cost, the growth and dividend potential of the enterprise is greater than the reported income. But typically no information

---

[22] *Ibid.*, p. 5.

is provided with respect to the magnitude or direction of the misstatement.

Rational investment decisions must be made on the basis of reasonable anticipations and investors must rely on the information contained in financial statements in forming those anticipations. As stated by George O. May:

> . . . whether the experience of a company in the recent past is likely to be repeated in the near future is practically immaterial if financial statements are to be considered as reports of stewardship or as guides to the profits that may properly be distributed. It is of paramount importance if they are to be used as a guide in determining whether to buy, hold, or sell securities.[23]

(8) PRICE-INDEX REPLACEMENT COST

Concept: The approximation of current replacement cost by the application of specific price indexes is intended to accomplish results similar to those derived from appraisal but with greater ease and objectivity and less cost of application. Replacement cost has been described as essentially a "cost method" in that the values would ordinarily be based directly on historical acquisition cost.

A distinction is sometimes made between *replacement* cost and *reproduction* cost, replacement cost referring to the cost of *equivalent* property and reproduction cost referring to the cost of *identical* property. The former is referred to here. Paton and Paton provide a lucid discussion of this point:

> It should be understood that the significant replacement cost is the cost of providing the existing

[23] George O. May, *Financial Accounting, A Distillation of Experience* (New York, The Macmillan Company, 1951), p. 21.

capacity to produce in terms of the most up-to-date methods available. Thus it's largely a waste of time to estimate the cost of replacing an obsolete or semiobsolete plant-unit literally in kind; such an estimate will neither afford a basis for a sound appraisal of the property nor furnish a useful measure of current operating cost. The fact of interest is what it would cost to replace the capacity represented in the existing asset with a machine of modern design. To put the point in another way, cost of replacing in kind is a significant basis on which to measure the economic importance of property in use only in the case of standard, up-to-date facilities.[24]

Attributes: The significance of replacement cost was explicitly acknowledged in part by the Committee on Accounting Procedure in Accounting Research Bulletin No. 33, issued in 1947:

> The committee recognizes that business management has the responsibility of providing for replacement of plant and machinery. It also recognizes that, in reporting profits today, the cost of material and labor is reflected in terms of "inflated" dollars while the cost of productive facilities in which capital was invested at a lower price level is reflected in terms of dollars whose purchasing power was much greater. There is no doubt that in considering depreciation in connection with product costs, prices, and business policies, management must take into consideration the probability that plant and machinery will have to be replaced at costs

---

[24] William A. Paton and William A. Paton, Jr., *Asset Accounting* (New York, The Macmillan Company, 1952), p. 325.

much greater than those of the facilities now in use.[25]

The rationale for the use of "price-index replacement cost" is identical with that for appraisal value. Again it is assumed that the balance sheet figures would have greater economic significance than unadjusted historical cost information. The major emphasis, however, is on sharpening the measurement of income by distinguishing between operating profits and exogenous gains and losses. Presumably the former are attributable to management and are more likely to be indicative of reasonable future expectations, while the latter tend to be less predictable and unrelated to dividend and growth potential.

Because "price index replacement costs" can be based on known and accepted published price indexes and historical acquisition costs, the method retains in full measure whatever objectivity advantage may properly be attributed to historical costs. It requires the use of certain computational techniques which are not particularly complicated but which do represent some additional "cost" of application compared to the use of unadjusted historical costs. It is assumed, however, that the cost of application is less than that involved in recurring appraisals. Any managerial influence which

---

[25] AICPA, Committee on Accounting Procedure, *Depreciation and High Costs,* Accounting Research Bulletin No. 33 (New York, AICPA, 1947), p. 267. The Committee concluded that increasing depreciation charges against income was not a satisfactory solution and recommended "annual appropriations of net income or surplus in contemplation of replacement of such facilities at higher price levels." This position was reiterated in 1953 in Accounting Research Bulletin No. 43 with six members dissenting. (Op. cit., pp. 67-71.)

might be reflected in the results of appraisals is precluded.

Edwards and Bell sum up the attributes of price-index replacement cost as follows:

> The use of indexes . . . to adjust known historic costs in order to estimate current costs of purchase implies the necessity of individual judgment, of course. So, too, does the estimation of an asset life and the establishment of a pattern for depreciation charges over the life of the asset. But we believe that (1) the derivation of current values for fixed assets can be accomplished on a consistent and objective basis with the information now available; (2) the quality of the information and the speed of reporting should improve if there is more extensive use of the data; (3) such estimates would be necessary only for some of the fixed assets held by the firm, i.e., only for those assets not currently marketed; (4) historic costs would be retained in the accounts; and (5) . . . adjustment on the basis of . . . [certain] indexes would make a substantial difference in the information available to managers and outsiders on operating gains and holding gains — for the decade 1947-1949 to 1957-1959, prices in general rose by only 15-18 per cent, but construction costs increased by 40 per cent, and the price of machinery rose by 50-70 per cent.[26]

---

[26] Edgar O. Edwards and Philip W. Bell, *The Theory and Measurement of Business Income* (Berkeley, University of California Press, 1961), pp. 187-188.